PRADO
MADRID

Newsweek/GREAT MUSEUMS OF THE WORLD

NEW YORK, N.Y.

**GREAT MUSEUMS
OF THE WORLD**

Editorial Director—Carlo Ludovico Ragghianti
Assistant—Giuliana Nannicini
Translation and Editing—Editors of ARTNEWS

Texts by:

Anna Pallucchini
Carlo Ludovicio Ragghianti
Licia Ragghianti Collobi

Design:

Fiorenzo Giorgi

Published by

NEWSWEEK, INC.
& ARNOLDO MONDADORI EDITORE

Library of Congress Catalog Card No. 68-20028

© 1968—Arnoldo Mondadori Editore—CEAM—Milan

© 1968—Photographs Copyright by Kodansha Ltd.—Tokyo

THE PRADO MUSEUM

F. J. SÁNCHEZ CANTÓN
Director

Quality rather than quantity is what distinguishes the Prado. There are museums in Europe which have a more complete representation of the various schools: they were formed by specialists and are the product of objective, art-historical criteria. But none of them surpasses the Prado's dazzling accumulation of paintings by masters from the 15th to 18th century.

A few statistics can serve as an introduction to a resume of its history and as an indication of its principal treasures, which include not only paintings but important collections of sculpture, drawings, jewelry of the Renaissance and the Baroque period, tapestries, medallions. etc. — although its paintings are the basis of the Prado's fame.

I

The latest *Catalogue of Paintings,* dated 1963, is the 33rd edition (the first appeared in 1819); it includes 2,164 works. That of *Sculpture* compiled by A. Blanco in 1957 lists 364 pieces. One on *Christian Art* by M. Lorente is being printed; the 120 jewels that constitute the so-called "Treasure of the Dauphin" were catalogued by D. Angulo (2nd edition, 1955). The drawings, approximately 4,000, are still being catalogued, except for the 485 Goyas published separately in 1952.

If the preceding data barely express the riches of the Prado, it will be more helpful perhaps to list some of the paintings of the great masters of Italy, Flanders, Holland, Germany, France and Spain. From Italy, the museum owns an admirable example of each of the following: Fra Angelico, Antonello da Messina and Mantegna: 8 Raphaels, 36 Titians, 13 Veroneses and 25 Tintorettos. Netherlandish painting of the 15th and 16th centuries includes 4 panels by the Master of Flémalle, 8 by van der Weyden, an equal number by Bosch, 4 by Patinir, 15 by Antonis Mor; among 17th century Flemish painters are 86 Rubens, 25 van Dycks, 43 Breughel de Velours, 39 Teniers; of the Germans 4 Dürers, 12 Mengs'; of the French 15 Poussins and 10 Claude Lorrains and, among the greatest painters of Spain: 35 El Grecos, plus two sculptures; 50 Velázquezes, the same number of Riberas, 40 Murillos and 118 Goyas apart from the drawings already mentioned.

Note that these proud statistics include no mention of works by such masters as Botticelli, Giorgione, Correggio, Luini, Andrea del Sarto, Lotto, the Bassani, the Carracci, Reni, Guercino, nor, among Northern artists, Bouts, Petrus Christus, van Orley, Gerard David, Mabuse, Massys, nor, from the 17th century, Rembrandt, van Ostade, Wouwermans, Fyt, Snyders, de Vos, Heda, nor, among Spanish painters, Gallego, Berruguete, Juanes, Morales, Sánchez Coello, Ribalta, Zurbaran, Alonso Cano, Juan Carreño, Claudio Coello, Valdés Leal, Luis Paret, Meléndez, V. Loper, all of whom figure in the Prado's collections.

The luster of most of these names and the quantity of their work owned by the museum gives some idea of its importance even before one knows its history and its significance in the history of art, and even after one has noticed that its collections include few Italian Primitives, 17th-century Dutch portraits and domestic interiors or few paintings of the English school. These are understandable deficiencies when one takes into account the way in which the Prado's basic collection was formed.

II

The history of the founding of the museum is closely linked with that of Spain through the 16th, 17th and 18th centuries, because basically it has been the national gallery of a unified country.

Even though kings from both Castile and Aragon showed a taste for miniatures and for paintings during the Middle Ages, the Prado can rarely exhibit examples from that period. Furthermore, the great unifying queen, Isabella the Catholic, owned numerous panels, of which 50 are still preserved in the Royal Palace of Madrid and the Royal Chapel of Granada, yet the Museum owns none of them. Her successors, from her grandson the Emperor Charles V to Ferdinand VII (who founded the Prado), followed her example in taking Spanish and foreign painters into their service, in commissioning works and in acquiring paintings by contemporary artists as well as earlier ones.

It is amazing to observe the abundance and the high quality of the art that the Spanish kings accumulated in their palaces. Especially notable are the taste and culture revealed by the acquisitions of Philip II and his nephew Philip IV. The former acquired works by Titian, Paolo Veronese, Tintoretto and El Greco, that is to say by the modern, daring painters of the day, and also by Hieronymus Bosch, Patinir, Massys, who were called "the strange ones." Although he was an absolute monarch and Flanders was the principal jewel of his crown, and although he profoundly admired the Ghent altarpiece by the van Eyck brothers, Philip resigned himself to commissioning Michel Coxcie to make a copy for the chapel of the Alcázar.

One of the basic characteristics of the Prado's collection appears here: its legitimacy. Even though proceeding from the royal collection and in spite of prolonged Spanish predominance in Europe, our masterpieces came to Spain by commission, by purchase, by gift or by inheritance.

The tastes of Philip IV, as revealed by his collecting, were no less selective. They were stimulated by the influence, or more precisely the friendship, of Velázquez. His connoisseurship is revealed in his relations with Rubens during the painter's second trip to Castile, and in the purchases he made in Antwerp from Ruben's estate after the artist's death. Further evidence of his interest may be found in the correspondence of the king with his Ambassador to London during the sale of the collections of King Charles I.

But there is a further proof of this predilection for beautiful paintings which is at the same time an eloquent indication of how Philip IV's plan to create a gallery of paintings in Madrid had already begun to take shape before the middle of the 17th century. Almost a century before that there had been talk of locating such a museum in the recently constructed royal palace of the Pardo near Madrid (now the residence of the Chief of State; it was partially destroyed by a fire on March 19, 1604). This early project never materialized, and Philip II gave more than 1,150 paintings to the Royal Monastery of St. Lawrence, the Escorial. Since it was for the most part open to the public and only 30 miles from Madrid, it more than satisfied the demands for study by artists and the curiosity of connoisseurs. Nevertheless the Escorial was insufficient for the extraordinary appetite for art of Philip IV who, according to the Aragonese painter Jusepe Martinez (he probably heard it from Velázquez), "proposed to found a gallery decorated with paintings and to seek out master painters so as to choose among their best pictures"; to which Velázquez replied: "I dare, Sir, to go to Rome and Venice to search for and to buy the best paintings that can be found . . ." He left, and after two long years during which Philip grew very impatient, he returned bringing notable acquisitions, but the museum project was never realized, neither in that century nor in the following one, despite enlightened spirits like the painter Mengs who, in a letter published by the traveler Ponz, expounded the idea of a picture gallery that could be installed in the new royal palace in Madrid — as though this idea had never occurred to anyone before.

As we have seen, the project had long preoccupied the court at Madrid as the collections grew through the centuries. The estimate made of the inventories of the royal palaces by the scholar P. Beroqui is amazing: King Charles II possessed 5,539 paintings at his death on November 1, 1700. These riches were seriously depleted in 1734 when the old Alcazar of Madrid burned; further losses were caused by the Wars of Succession and of Independence, losses for which Philip V and Charles III tried to compensate with new purchases. The latter while still a prince bought a large number of paintings, among them the *Cardinal* by Raphael.

One could say that all 11 Spanish kings who ruled during three centuries had a passion for buying paintings.

It has been proved by historical texts that it was not difficult to obtain permission to study or see the royal collections, but what proves it most of all are the principal schools of painting which flourished in Spain: neither the Toledan nor Valencian school at the end of the 16th and beginning of the 17th centuries could have been formed without knowledge of the paintings acquired for Madrid and the Escorial, nor the Sevillan nor Madrilenian school of the 17th century without a profound knowledge of Venetian and Flemish works on exhibit in the capital.

The credit must be given to the kings: great collectors of admirable paintings.

III

It was to the German painter Anton Raphael Mengs, the principal artist at the court of Charles III (who had inherited the Spanish throne at 43 after a 20 year reign in Naples), that one must attribute the monarch's favorable attitude toward the arts and sciences: he dedicated a building to house the Royal Academy of Noble Arts of San Fernando — to put "under one roof" the collections of arts and objects of the natural sciences; he inaugurated the Botanical Garden in the Prado of the Monastery of San Jeronimo el Real; and ordered the construction of the adjoining museum, a commission given to the Neo-Classical architect Don Juan de Villaneuva, who submitted plans on May 30, 1785. The underlying idea of the building was not understood until 1962 when Prof. Rumeu de Armas published "The Political Testament of the Count of Floridablanca" (the most illustrious Spanish governor of his time) and showed that the building was first destined to accommodate both the fine arts and the natural sciences. But by the end of the 18th century, the construction of the Prado was not much advanced, the delay being caused perhaps in part by the death of Charles III in December, 1788. On the other hand, the project to found a picture gallery began to take life, in theory at any rate, early in the new century.

The proposal presented to the Constituent Assembly by Bertrand Barère on May 26, 1791, for the creation of the Louvre museum helped to stimulate the order given by the Minister Urquijo on September 1, 1800, to bring from Seville to Madrid "paintings by Murillo, a measure conforming to the practice of all the civilized nations of Europe where steps are being taken to establish schools and museums in the seat of the Court." That the project was constantly gaining momentum is proved by the fact that in the order of Godoy, revoking that of Urquijo, a "Museum of the King" is mentioned.

The Napoleonic invasion of Spain with its usurpation of the Spanish throne by Joseph Bonaparte crystallized these diffused projects, and in a decree signed by Urquijo on August 20, 1809, a Museum of Paintings was created in Madrid, assembling works from many public establishments including the royal palaces. By another decree two days later, the Palace of Buenavista was designated as the home of this project (the palace today is part of the Defense Ministry). The "Joseph Museum," as it has been called, barely advanced beyond the project stage, but part of the collection that was confiscated from Godoy was left in Buenavista as well as some paintings from abolished monasteries and convents, but civil wars prevented further realization of the scheme.

Meanwhile, the construction of the Prado continued. In 1806 (the dating is not certain), it seems that work was well advanced. During the occupation of Madrid by the French, the ground floor was utilized for stables (a poet cried: "Its royal salons/ in vile uses were profaned"), and also parts of the gutters were pulled off. All of which explains why, when the Ambassador of Napoleon in Madrid (Conde de la Porest) wrote to Paris mentioning a meeting of the Council of State about the Prado Museum (September 20, 1811), *"un sourire général"* was raised since the Prado was considered unfit for formal use. Nobody then was able to predict its future.

12

IV

The end of the Peninsular War and the return of Ferdinand VII to the throne saw a return to the project of the "intruder King," i.e. the establishment of a national museum for paintings, including those from the suppressed convents in the Buenavista Palace and those in the Academy of Fine Arts. But the idea was never realized because the reopened convents demanded their art back, and the Buenavista Palace required extensive repairs.

The Council of Castile expressed its opinion in favor of a royal project for a museum to be organized in "the famous building which was constructed for this purpose at an expense of many millions . . in the paseo of the Prado." The same year that the king entered Madrid, he dictated an order accepting the proposal of the Council, on December 26, 1814.

The two years which followed Ferdinand VII's wedding (his second marriage) to his niece, the Portuguese Infanta Maria Isabel, on September 29, 1816, until her death on December 26, 1818, were decisive for the restoration and completion of the Prado Museum, thanks to the help of the short-lived queen. An official text in March of the same year, in addition to other evidence, states that Count Floridablanca's idea that "the sciences and the arts united would take on new life" continued to develop, and I can add that during the years 1922–32 a stuffed bird of prey perched in some branches, although very moth-eaten, was still on exhibition in a showcase. But one should note that the public galleries of the Museum exhibited only works of art.

The Prado was inaugurated on November 19, 1819. The installation was limited to the rotunda of the main floor and to lateral wings divided into three halls. Not more than only paintings of living or recently deceased artists were shown: Goya, José Madrazo, etc. All the paintings belonged to the Royal Patrimony, and the directors for the first 20 years were aristocrats. The collection grew rapidly. After two years the 311 works in the first catalogue had swelled to 512 in the second, thanks to the installation of the Italian school in the Great Gallery. After six years the museum had acquired considerable riches, always to the detriment of the royal palaces: the 1828 catalogue numbers 755 paintings. It would be tiresome and not very useful in the present context to continue the numerical list of new acquisitions.

V

An architectural study of the building — a jewel of Spanish Neo-Classic art — has been made in an excellent monograph by F. Chueca (Madrid, 1952). What has been said about the nobility of its lines and proportions is well deserved, but the undeniable aptness of Villanueva's construction as a museum of paintings has not always been recognized: the dimensions of the rooms, the height of the walls, the number and placement of intervals — nothing is overwhelming or overpowering.

One should add (as a traveler from Cadiz, Count de Maule, pointed out around

1806) that it was expected that Villaneuva, "after its conclusion would present to the public plans and designs giving a precise description of such a beautiful work"; but the death of the architect and the turbulent years for Spain which followed perhaps explain the fact that such precious documents have not survived. The Prado Museum has on occasion afforded surprises to those who work there and who know it. Thus in 1930 we "discovered" the magnificent rotunda of the ground floor, a superb piece of architecture then without a comfortable access, which in the 18th century could not have had natural light, yet was nevertheless surely intended to be visited and adorned with works of art since it contains four niches. In addition, during the reconstruction of the rotunda on the main floor in 1964, we found, hidden in the woodwork, a ringlike space around the hemisphere with a heavy stone cornice, on the ringlike vault of the rotunda. The discovery of Villanueva's records might clarify these mysteries.

Another special quality of this beautiful building is the additions made during the 19th and 20th centuries, which fit without violating the whole, to the lasting credit of the architects López Agusdo, Arnal, Grases, F. Arbós, P. de Muguruza, M. Lorente, F. Chueca and J. M. de Muguruza, authors of the complements and additions to the work of Villanueva.

The museum continued to thrive and grow at the expense of the Royal collections until the autumn of 1868 when the triumph of the Revolution nationalized it. For 30 years its directors had continued to amass paintings and the catalogue of 1843, which is the work of Pedro de Madrazo, son of José, who was a director of the museum, includes 1,833 paintings; it was basically the same volume which was re-edited until 1920.

The principal novelty in the life of the museum was the creation on June 7, 1912, of the Board of Patronage, which directs it and which immediately began expanding the building with an addition of 24 rooms completed between 1917 and 1920. Then followed the re-design of the main gallery and the construction of a central staircase in 1923–27. In 1955–56, two new wings with a total of 16 rooms were added; in 1963–64, six more were built; presently work has begun on an extension of equal size.

VI

The essential change caused in the museum when it ceased to depend on the Royal Patrimony (and the collections of the Spanish kings) and became the organism of a Ministry, soon resulted in an additional, satellite museum, "The Trinity," named for the order of the former Madrid convent. Its collection, more piled-up than installed, was composed of paintings from suppressed monasteries and convents. There was little room for these or other additions in the Prado and so the museum soon began to distribute paintings on deposit to provincial museums, universities, official offices, etc. But at the same time paintings of certain periods and schools which had been lacking began to enter the collections, including Spanish panels of the 15th and 16th centuries.

The lack of such works in the royal collections, which was beginning to be remedied with the incorporation of the "Trinity" treasures, has been one of the concerns of the Board of Patronage since its creation; today the Prado possesses a good representation (even though incomplete) of Medieval and Renaissance peninsular art which, though related to the Northern "International Style" and to the Flemish and Italian Renaissance, presents vigorous and original characteristics. Notable examples of 12th century mural paintings are also on show.

After what has been said about the origins of the royal collection, it is hardly necessary to insist on the dazzling richness of the total collection, formed by the Italian paintings (the Venetians in particular), by the Netherlandish school with its Gothic fantasy, the Flanders of Rubens and his followers and the 16th to 18th century Spaniards, from El Greco to Goya.

The Board of Patronage was faced with a total absence of English painting and with a small representation of the 17th century Dutch school, easy to explain by the friction between Spain and both countries due to religious and political questions. As has been said, another area poorly represented in the palace collections and, as a consequence, in the Prado, is Italy prior to Raphael. Although it was not easy to fill these gaps, persistent efforts have provided the Prado with a hall of English portraits and some examples which complement aspects of the Dutch school. Good fortune has also graced the museum with eight early Italian panels.

The Prado with its treasures of amazing quality and quantity, despite certain gaps, constitutes one of the finest collections for the study of the course of European painting; it possesses not only the most beautiful examples of the Venetian School in its triumphal moment with "the poems" of Titian and the most varied collection of the mythological and religious creations of Rubens, but also the strictest lessons of Velázquez' and Ribera's confrontation with reality. And if this were not enough to ensure the glory of the Prado, it embodies the liberating flow away from conventions and formulas seen in the diverse explorations of Bosch, Patinir, El Greco and Goya.

F. J. Sánchez Cantón

ITALY

ANDREA MANTEGNA. *The Death of the Virgin.*

The upper part of this work was mutilated before it reached the Prado. The missing section represented Christ — enclosed in a sort of wrapping of clouds spangled with cherubim against a background of a vault in the architectural style of Alberti — receiving the soul of the Virgin. A fragment has been found in the Vendeghini Collection in Ferrara. Therefore, we can reconstruct the work, aided by the knowledge of a similar iconographic solution in the mosaic of the Mascoli Chapel in St. Mark's, Venice. Various suggestions have been proposed for the relationship between this picture and the mosaic, but critics now believe that the mosaic was a derivation from the Madrid panel, which from its style may be dated around 1460. There is no exact documentation on the work, but it is probable that it was part of the decoration of the chapel in the Castello di S. Giorgio, which Mantegna began for the Gonzaga family around 1459, and which also included the beautiful panels now in the Uffizi. In the 19th century these were reunited to form a triptych, with the *Adoration of the Magi* in the center, and the *Circumcision* and the *Ascension* at the sides. By 1460, Mantegna had completed his youthful Paduan experience and was preparing for his masterpiece in the Camera degli Sposi in Mantua. In our small panel the virtuosity of the epic narrator is transformed into an emotional tension that finds expression in the highly composed structure of the circle of Apostles around the bier (only broken by the figure leaning forward and swinging a thurible over the body of the Virgin), and in the chromatic force of every detail. It was the mellowness of color and perhaps the crystalline luminosity of the landscape elements (a dam on the lake of Mantua?) that suggested Bellini as an author to Adolfo Venturi. This unsustainable hypothesis had a reasonable aspect. It is in the five years between 1456 and 1460 that Bellini was observing Mantegna most attentively, as is proven by his *Transfiguration* in the Museo Correr, which was considered to be by Mantegna.

SANDRO BOTTICELLI. *Nastagio degli Onesti.* p. 20

This illustration of a scene in a Boccaccio story was commissioned for the marriage of Giannozzo Pucci and Lucrezia Bini (1483), as indicated by the coats of arms; stylistic examination confirms this dating. The series of panels is by Botticelli in concept and design, but the execution is mainly studio work and critics recognize in it the collaboration of Bartolomeo di Giovanni. Botticelli had come back from Rome in 1482 famous for the work he had done there and, overloaded with commissions, was obliged to hire assistants. Certainly the drawing is very fine — "all alive with delicate and pungent graces" (Bettini) — and reflects the narrative ability of the master and his penetrating intuition in translating the original novella. In it, Boccaccio tells the tale of an unrequited lover who changes his lady's mind: he made her visualize hell, and the perpetual torment of a cruel woman by the lover who had suffered damnation for her. In the detail reproduced here, the youth is seen pursuing the nude girl; he knocks her to the ground, tears out her heart, throws it to his dogs, then starts the pursuit and torture again, the cycle continuing through eternity. Without question it is the most beautiful of the panels. The space deepens from the shore of Classe to the farther reaches of the marine view; the distant horizon divides the surface into

18

ANDREA MANTEGNA
Isola di Carturo 1431 — Mantua 1506
The Death of the Virgin (ca. 1460)
Panel; 21 1/4″ × 16 1/2″ Provenance: collection of Charles I, King of England.

SANDRO BOTTICELLI
Florence 1445 — Florence 1510
Nastagio degli Onesti (1483)
Detail. Panel; 2'8" × 4'6". One of a series of panels for a nuptial chamber, executed for the marriage of Giannozzo Pucci and Lucrezia Bini (in 1483). With two other episodes, it comes from the Cambó collection in Barcelona.

two areas equal in size and different in intention. And the space is scanned with a certain regularity by the verticals of the pines supporting their green domes. The elegant figures move amid these geometric coordinates, and the fantastic narration is achieved effortlessly in a play of intricate rhythms.

RAPHAEL. *The Madonna of the Fish.*

Nothing is known of how Raphael was commissioned to do this outstanding work. A letter of Summonte, in 1524, indicates that it was then in the chapel of the del Doce or del Duca family in S. Domenico, Naples. It is reasonable to think that it was conceived as an ex-voto for the cure of an eye malady, as is suggested by the presence of Tobias, who is being presented to the Virgin by the Archangel Raphael, and of St. Jerome. Raphael composed the group with a knowledge of curvilinear rhythms that recall the disposition of the figures around the arches in S. Maria della Pace (1514). The figures, however, appear exalted, purified in their reverent approach to the solemn, somewhat cold-looking Virgin, who leaves the principal role to the Child, seen in the act of grasping at the sacred book from which St. Je-

RAPHAEL
Urbino 1482 — Rome 1520
The Madonna of the Fish (ca. 1514)
Canvas (transfered from panel); 7' × 5'2".
Provenance: S. Domenico, Naples, where it remained until 1638; the Duke of Medina, Spanish Viceroy, moved it to Madrid in 1644; the next year it entered the collection of Philip IV.

rome raises his eyes, and leaning affectionately toward the group of the angel and Tobias. The work is not considered to be entirely by the master's hand. Taking into account its less than excellent state of preservation, it is still an outstanding example of the formal and refined "prose" that Raphael knew how to compose during the years in which he created the Stanza of the Fire in the Borgo (1514–16).

RAPHAEL. *Portrait of a Cardinal.*

Masterpiece of Raphael's portrait painting in the first years of his activity in Rome, it is considered contemporary with the Stanza della Segnatura. In particular it is comparable to the fresco of Julius II, in the guise of Gregory IX, approving the decretals delivered to him by St. Raymond of Pennafort — a fresco that cannot be dated after 1511. Raphael's vocation for portraiture was revealed in his earliest work. In the frescoes of the Vatican Stanzas — that poem of human spirituality — numerous portraits of friends and famous personalities of the time appear as historical figures of the past. But despite innumerable suggestions by scholars (the candidates most frequently proposed are Alidosi and Ippolito d'Este), the impenetrable face of this cardinal has managed to maintain its incognito. The impression made by those sealed lips becomes emblematic of the history of this memorable image, which out of its anonymity attains the universality of a human type: the calculating and enigmatic diplomat.

The formal means by which the figure of the cardinal is achieved verges on overstatement. It has been observed that the composition consists of two inverted pyramids joined at their apexes, and shows that play of volumes as perfect forms, almost an obsession in Renaissance painting. And other subtle harmonies have been noted in the play of line that defines the face and the hat. Certainly the impression created of a sense of incorruptible matter — the stuff of which the image is made — emphasizes admirably the inflexible spirituality that must have emanated from the illustrious, aristocratic model.

ANDREA DEL SARTO. *The Sacrifice of Abraham.*   p. 24

Vasari relates that Andrea del Sarto, on the suggestion of a Florentine friend who sold art works to Francis I, King of France, made a beautiful *Sacrifice of Abraham* (now in Dresden) and executed a smaller but equally perfect replica for Paolo da Terrarossa. The subsequent vicissitudes of the two pictures become very complicated in Vasari's account, but evidently the version in the Prado is the second one, given its size (a sketch for it is in the Cleveland Museum).

It is undoubtedly a late work, with a certain strength and an ordered quality. Vasari mentions with admiration "the very handsome and tender child Isaac, all nude, trembling with fear of death," the boy's robes fallen to the ground that are "real and natural" and finally the unusual landscape. If the work is read according to such naturalistic standards, the painting is certainly notable. To our sensibilities, however, the bombast in Abraham's gesture is inescapable, even accepting the intention of creating space. Nor is the excessive balance of the somewhat academic design entirely acceptable, even if we recognize a more agitated handling — a Pontormo-like sensibil-

RAPHAEL
Portrait of a Cardinal (1509–1510)
Panel; 2'7" × 2'.

JACOPO TINTORETTO
Venice 1518 — Venice 1594
The Finding of Moses (ca. 1550–1555)
Canvas; 1'10" × 3'11". Bought in Venice by
Velázquez for King Philip IV.

JACOPO TINTORETTO
Joseph and Potiphar's Wife (ca. 1550–1555)
Canvas; 1'9 1/4" × 3'10". Bought in Venice
by Velázquez for Philip IV.

It is perhaps useful to recall that the taste for epic descriptions, for battles, which in the succeeding century became a true and proper genre, had its enthusiastic pioneers: it was in 1581 that Tasso published his celebrated poem, *Gerusalemme Liberata*.

JACOPO TINTORETTO. *The Finding of Moses.*
With six other biblical scenes — *Judith and Holofernes, Susanna and the Elders, The Queen of Sheba before Solomon, Esther before Ahasuerus, Joseph and Potiphar's Wife, The Purification of the Midianite Virgins* (unfortunately damaged and repainted) — it made up the decoration of a ceiling in a palace in Venice, where Velázquez bought them, during his second Venetian sojourn, for Philip IV. The centerpiece must have been the *Purification of the Midianite Virgins,* as the Spanish historian, Palomino de Castro, clearly states; the other rectangular canvases formed a frieze around it. The decorative sumptuousness of the paintings, the illusionistic perspective frameworks and the rich color call for a fairly early dating: the years between 1550 and 1555, when Tintoretto came closest to Paolo Veronese. This work in particular, with its harmonious rhythm of the figures linked by broad curvilinear cadences echoed by the branches bending over the group in which Moses is at dead center, reminds us of Veronese's modules. Though these stem from Mannerism, they are quieted by the instinct for equilibrium typical of Paolo, in whom Tintoretto found inspiration at this moment.

We are far from the violence of the first perspective experiments inspired by Mantuan examples, which Tintoretto had carried out in the notable series of ceiling paintings for a Venetian palace — a series that is now in the Galleria Estense, Modena.

JACOPO TINTORETTO. *Joseph and Potiphar's Wife.*
This painting is one of the smaller parts of the frieze that decorated the ceiling of a Venetian palace, from which it was bought with the other six canvases in the same series by Velázquez, who had been sent by Philip IV to Italy to acquire pictures for the Royal Collection. The Spanish master must have been particularly pleased by the richness and luminosity of the work and the immediacy with which the brush translates the mental image of the artist on to the canvas.

The composition is felicitous — asymmetrical, mobile and constructed around two divergent lines created by the velvet curtain and the figure of Joseph, who pulls violently away from the beautiful reclining nude. The perspective construction, by which the composition is seen from a very low viewpoint, creates a slight feeling of vertigo. It is this idea of space that typifies Tintoretto's creative character. If it is Mannerism, in particular through his relationship to Giulio Romano in Mantua, that gives the Venetian painter the means for these flights of imagination, we also must recognize that Tintoretto makes use of it admirably. He rendered his own spiritual anxiety as well as that of his time. To return to an analysis of the color, whose quality is so high in this moment of contact with Veronese, one is struck by the nude Potiphar's wife, defined by a sinuous but tense line, which emanates an extraordinary luminosity counterpointed by the dark green of the alcove and the silken materials that are traversed by shining flickers.

47

PAOLO VERONESE. *Venus and Adonis.*

Certainly a genius in painting, Paolo Veronese maintained from the beginning to the end of his career a number of constant factors. As interpreter of certain aspirations of the culture of his time, he risked alienation from the deepest and most uneasy currents of 16th century spirituality, pursuing his own ideal of formal perfection, which in the end is an escape. The last of Paolo's production (1570–88), however, is touched by a breath of pathos and reflects the need for meditation, which is evident not only in his choice of themes but in the evolution of his style. But noble images were also produced in this period, such as the allegorical fables painted for Rudolph II and this idyll of Venus and Adonis. "The two protagonists are lost in the same enchantment as Tasso's Rinaldo and Amida," as R. Pallucchini says. And this is true especially for the enchanted atmosphere in which the artist immersed his figures: the diaphanously luminous Venus, Adonis relaxed in sleep, Cupid holding back the impatient dog. There is not, however, as in Tasso's poetry, a dramatic motive to Paolo Veronese's escapism. To appreciate this it is enough to compare the thematic development of Titian's *Venus and Adonis,* with its presentiment of death, and the somewhat fatuous gesture of Venus waving her fan and watching over her sleeping lover in Paolo's version. Certainly his classical inclinations, after the dissipation of his energies as a colorist in such canvases as the *Marriage of St. Catherine* and the *Rape of Europa* in the Palazzo Ducale, here again recover their beautiful equilibrium.

PAOLO VERONESE. *The Finding of Moses.* *p. 50*

This small painting is the twin of one in the National Gallery of Washington, even to the dimensions. It must have been much admired, as there are other replicas — although none on this high level — which are in the museums of Dresden and Dijon. It is certainly later than the Prado's *Venus and Adonis.* The dimensions themselves permit the painter an intensity of exceptional color effects, without however reaching the feeling of satiety noticeable in some of the preceding courtly compositions.

The charm of Paolo Veronese's rare small-sized compositions, which were created for refined patrons, could be compared to a musician, accustomed to the symphonic power of the organ, improvising delicate variations on a spinet. To continue the musical metaphor, the composition flows along in continuously legato rhythms, from the figure of the slave to the young girl handing the child to Pharaoh's daughter and her elderly companion, while three other figures at the right repeat the stepped succession of the group. The counterpoint in color is varied and rich. A diverting note is the portrayal of the Egyptian city, with temples, towers and pinnacles — a fantasy spun from the complicated sensibilities of Mannerism.

GIOVAN BATTISTA MORONI. *Portrait.* *p. 51*

Although the activity of Moroni, disciple of Moretto da Brescia, includes religious scenes, the painter's fame is connected with the series of portraits he executed during his Brescian period, which lasted until 1553, as well as after his return to Bergamo, where he acquired a vast clientele. Titian himself recommended Moroni for his "naturalness" to a gentleman of the Al-

PAOLO VERONESE
Verona 1528 — Venice 1588
Venus and Adonis (ca. 1570–1575)
Canvas; 6'11 1/2" ×6'4 1/4". Acquired by
Velázquez in Venice for Philip IV.

GIOVAN BATTISTA MORONI
Albino (Bergamo) 1523? — Albino 1578
Portrait (ca. 1560)
Canvas; 3'10 3/4" × 2'11 3/4". In 1666 it
figures in a list of paintings in the Alcazar,
Madrid.

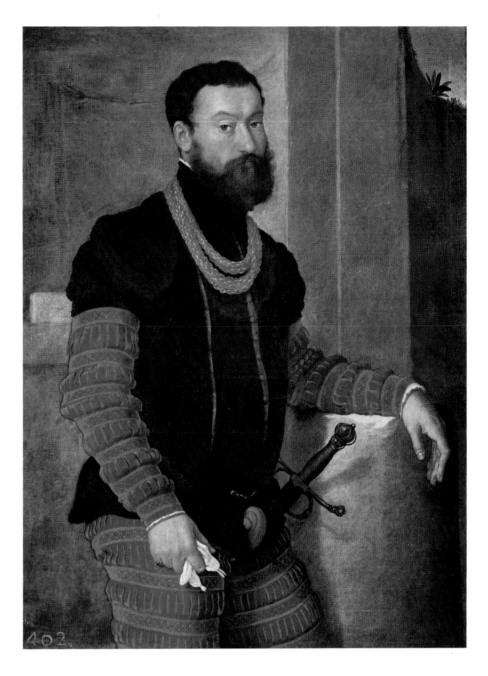

PAOLO VERONESE
The Finding of Moses (1570–1575)
Canvas; 19 3/4" × 17". From the collection
of Philip IV.

bani family. In fact it is inescapable that he has a particular ability to approach reality directly, which goes back to a Lombard tradition and relates him to other great contemporary artists of similar experience but belonging to the Venetian world: Lotto, Savoldo and Romanino. Some compositions in the Mannerist taste appear to have been filtered through Venetian styles, as in the *Portrait of a Poet,* 1560, in the Pinacoteca Tosio Martinengo, Brescia. Our portrait is considered to be of the same period. In Moroni's gallery of personalities, who are for the most part unknown, but who reveal their social positions and specific trades or professions — the tailor, the lawyer — this one is considered "the official." A consciousness of authority emanates from the personage, from his golden collar that stands out on the rich garb, from the severity of the entire composition, both from the point of view of color and from the sober architectural reference.

51

GIAMBATTISTA TIEPOLO. *The Immaculate Conception.*

On March 31, 1762, Tiepolo left for Madrid with his sons Domenico and Lorenzo, on the invitation of Charles III, to fresco the throne room. This demanding commission was successfully carried out and the Venetian was asked to decorate other halls. Then there seems to have been a halt in Tiepolo's production in 1765–66, and in 1767 the painter asked the court for more work. Despite the obvious hostility of the King's Confessor, Padre de Electa, and the manifest rivalry of other painters — among them Mengs — he obtained an order to execute seven large canvases for the church of S. Pascual de Aranjuez. *The Immaculate Conception* belongs to this series, which is religious not only in iconographic theme but also in interior motivation. The subject was not new to Tiepolo. He took up again the iconography of the altarpiece now in the museum of Vicenza: a representation of the Virgin as a celestial being crushing underfoot a serpent that is attacking the earth, while angels adore her. A stylistic comparison throws light on the evolution of Tiepolo's style in the last years of his career. In the Vicenza altarpiece, datable around 1735, the Virgin is solidly constructed, following a module of Piazzetta's. Her white garment seems to emit flashes, and the violence of the light and shade also throws the soft limbs of the cupids into strong relief. In the Madrid picture, all violence is gone. Light emanates without combustion and discreet little angels lean adoringly from the soft cloud. The ascending motion of the Virgin is accentuated, and around her the mantle swells and palpitates, like a sail filling with wind. A very fine sketch for the painting is in London, in the collection of Lord Kinnaird.

GIAMBATTISTA TIEPOLO
Venice 1696 — Madrid 1770
The Immaculate Conception (ca. 1767–1769)
Canvas; 9′2″ × 4′11 3/4″. Signed: *"Dn. Juan Batta Tiepolo inv. et pinx."* Painted for the church of San Pascual of Aranjuez. In the Prado since 1828.

GIAMBATTISTA TIEPOLO. *The Triumph of Venus.*   p. 54

We do not know whether this splendid sketch served for the execution of a ceiling for the "Court of Muscovy" on which Tiepolo worked in the autumn of 1761, a year before his departure for Spain. Stylistically it is close to the sketches for the Madrid ceilings, which are now in the museums of Cambridge and Boston. If our sensibility occasionally finds it difficult to enjoy the spectacular ability of Tiepolo in his grand fresco compositions, and if this awkward feeling is complicated by thoughts on the character of the painter, who was devoted to the exaltation of unstable powers and discredited myths, our reservations fall away before the felicity of his sketches. The ability of the Venetian tradition to achieve with color and light a semblance of reality and absolute creations of the imagination found its last incarnations in the magisterial quality of Tiepolo's forms and in the lyricism of Guardi's *vedute*. Venus goes by lounging in a carriage drawn by doves and escorted by cupids. Mercury, sketched in a few rapid strokes, descends from on high, while Minerva and Saturn below, seen against a white wall which accentuates the perspective, observe the procession. The most enchanting passage is that of the Three Graces who, from their throne of white clouds, offer their rosy nudity to our view. Here again is the miracle of a light that does not destroy but exalts form, that does not imitate reality but transfigures it. A fine engraving of the composition was executed by Tiepolo's son Lorenzo.

Page 54:
GIAMBATTISTA TIEPOLO
The Triumph of Venus (ca. 1726–1765)
Canvas; 2′9″ × 2′ 1/4″. Sketch for a lost ceiling; in the Prado since 1834.

SPAIN

THE MASTER OF ZAFRA. *St. Michael the Archangel.*

The signature on the sword is believed to be that of the armorer. The work has been attributed to the painter Juan Sanchez de Castro or a follower of his, but with little basis. There are Flemish elements in the band of angels and in the diabolical figures below, which recall Bosch, but do not have his crystalline details. A Flemish manner is also evident in the large figure of the Archangel, but the regular forms of the armor and head also suggest an Italian influence. The determining factor is the composition, which is clearly and rigorously architectonic even in the rich imagery that crowds the margins of the panel. The oblong form is divided by two diagonals on which is constructed the straddling figure of the Archangel; this is closed off above in an angular arrangement, around which rotates a large ellipse descending from the mantle to the wing of the infernal dragon below. Despite the dense pulsation of the little figures emerging on every side, this simple, immediate format — which allows the viewer to follow the central figure in its surging upward development — sums up the whole image. In the mirroring center of the shield is reflected the lateral scene in which a demon and a guardian angel fight for the soul of the donor of the work. The Master of Zafra is certainly one of the best artists working in Spain around 1475, and his technical performance has a rare refinement.

BARTOLOMÉ DE CARDENAS BERMEJO. *San Domingo de Silos.*

The stylistic language of Bartolomé Bermejo is clearly Flemish, from his first known work (a *St. Michael* now in the Ludlow collection), to the *Pietà* in the Cathedral of Barcelona, dated 1490. The place and nature of his training, and perhaps also his early activity, are to be sought among the artists of Tournai and of Rogier, and immediately afterwards in the vicinity of Dirk Bouts (1420–75). Bouts's influence is seen in this magnificent *San Domingo* enthroned within a Gothic construction decorated with fabulous towers, pinnacles and niches containing the seven cardinal Virtues — Strength, Justice, Charity, Prudence, Temperance, Faith and Hope, in the form of women sumptuously dressed in multicolored robes. The figure of St. Dominick, the great promoter of the Faith, with his book and elaborately worked pastoral, is presented in a strict frontal position and is constructed from triangles, in accordance with the canons of Gothic architecture. The cope embroidered with figures, with its thickness and weight, accentuates the impression of a large statue placed on the imposing carved throne; and above, the jeweled mitre starts the upward surge of the spires. In other works the dominating preference is for intensely dramatic and agitated subjects, like the *Descent into Limbo* (in the museum in Barcelona), which recalls Bouts's infernos, with their shrieking nudes and monsters. In this panel everything is apparently motionless — to create the majesty of an icon — but the various elements and details, worked up with almost unflagging exasperation, show the character of the master's imagination. With Nuño Gonçalvez he was among the greatest Iberian artists of his time.

56

THE MASTER OF ZAFRA
St. Michael the Archangel (ca. 1475)
Tempera on panel; 7'11 1/4" × 5'1/4".
Provenance: Hospital of San Miguel, Zafra (Andalusia); acquired by the Prado in 1924.

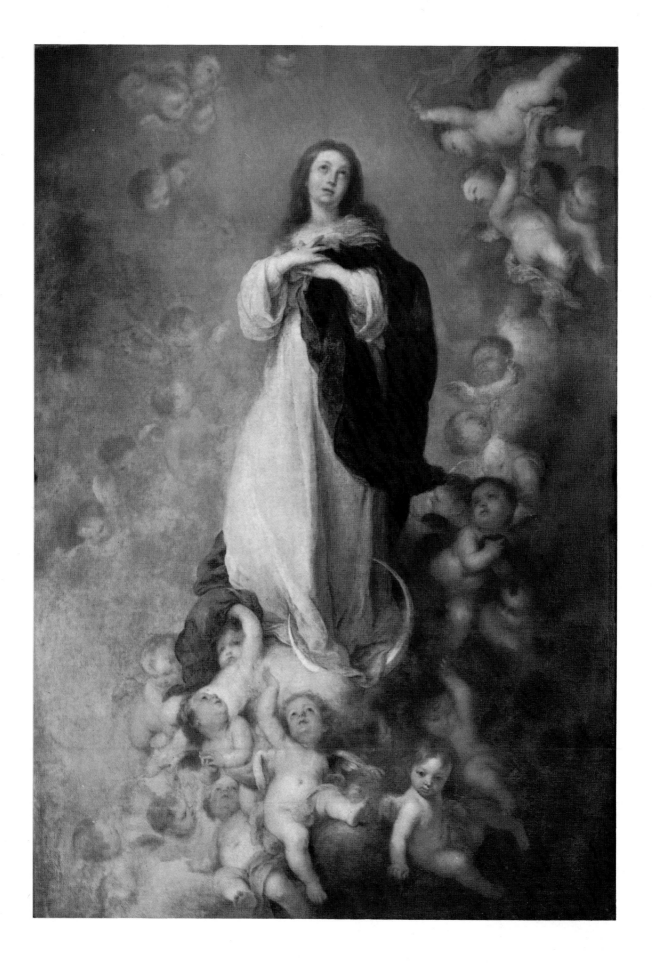

BARTOLOMÉ ESTEBAN MURILLO
Holy Family (del Pajarito)
Oil on canvas; 4'8 3/4" × 6'2". In the
collection of Isabella Farnese at
La Granja. Taken to Paris by Joseph I;
restored to the Prado in 1818.

BARTOLOMÉ ESTEBAN MURILLO
Seville 1618 — Seville 1682
The Immaculate Conception
Oil on canvas; 7'3 1/2" × 3'10 1/2". Painted
in 1678 for the Hospital de los Venerables
in Seville; stolen by Maréchal Soult, entered
the Louvre; subsequently returned to Spain.

BARTOLOMÉ ESTEBAN MURILLO. *The Immaculate Conception.*
In this late work, it is clear that Murillo looked to Guido Reni for the "sentimental" faces and to van Dyck for technique. The painting, however, is among the most integrated and successful of his last period, with its atmospheric density animated by suffused gleams, and the light figures enveloped in a luminous haze. Never leaving Madrid, Murillo picked up at a distance and through various intermediaries what was going on in contemporary painting, and after an early neo-Caravaggesque period influenced by Ribalta, Ribera and Zurbaran, he turned to Reni, Rubens and van Dyck. His production was vast, alternating works of a marked "realistic" character with others in which the accent of devotion does not concern only the religious themes, but also the manner of painting. Murillo has long been appreciated and famous, even more than his other great contemporaries, for his masterly expression. In works with a strong literary or religious content, his undoubted talent is not always accompanied by the lyric accent that is found in his penetrating portraits or in his intimate representations of ordinary life.

BARTOLOMÉ ESTEBAN MURILLO. *Holy Family (del Pajarito).*
Painted around 1650, it is among the works that still show Murillo close to Zurbaran and Ribera. In this domestic scene the emphasis is on its character as a playful interlude, without any sacred feeling. The composition intelligently adopts the counterpoised blocked-out masses of the Caravaggesque heritage, and the diagonal relationships, which are however attenuated in a composed but fluent dialogue of forms. In this work of his early maturity, Murillo also shows his qualities as an ingratiating designer of scenes keyed to a sentiment between the religious and the commonplace, in an atmosphere of softly indulgent devotion, which is well served by his pictorial skill.

BARTOLOMÉ ESTEBAN MURILLO.   *Rebecca and Eleazar.*

Typical of Murillo's middle period is the taste for Ribera and the references to Reni. The Biblical scene takes place on a stage immediately presented to the spectator and is developed in the arc of figures around the cylindrical well. The handling of the terra-cotta amphora emphasizes the divergence of directions, and the compositional bridge between Eleazar and the group of women is clear and simple. In the background to the left, in the road in the valley, a caravan waits in sunlight, a device frequent in Murillo. The color, especially in the marginal areas, preserves the smoky contrasts of Ribera, but in the polite, somewhat idealized figures of the women, it is enlivened by pleasingly liquid as well as ringing notes. The high, sometimes conventional, professionalism typical of many of Murillo's works, is surpassed in this calm, intimate and luminous performance.

It is typical of the artist, in this as in other representations of sacred themes (the Mosaic and Christological scenes in La Caridad, Seville, 1670–74), to shift the main interest to genre aspects, refining and rendering affable representations of the contemporary world, especially the peasant's. There is a

BARTOLOMÉ ESTEBAN MURILLO
Rebecca and Eleazar
Oil on canvas; 3'6 1/4" ×5'7 1/4". Acquired in Seville by Isabella Farnese in 1733, then in the collection at La Granja (1766); subsequently entered the Prado. Executed around 1650.

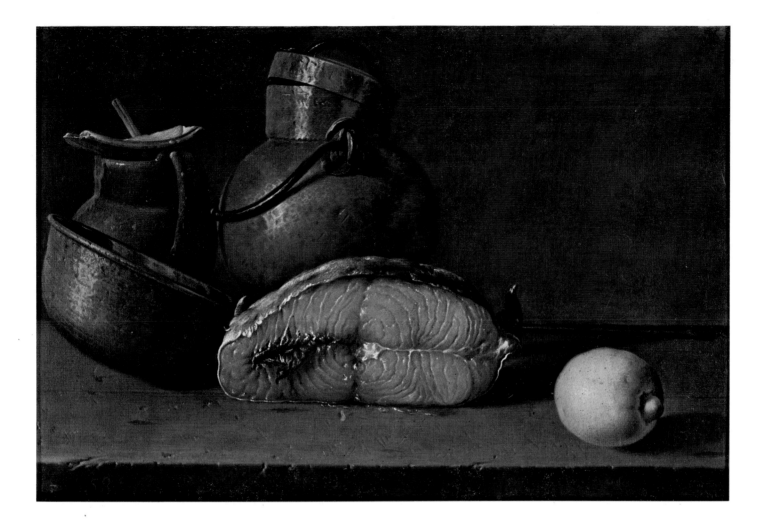

sentimental inflection which, declining from an intentionally realistic point of departure toward the crudely pictorial (as in the beggars), would be appreciated by the pastoral Arcadians of the following century.

LUIS EUGENIO MELÉNDEZ. *Still-life with Salmon and Lemon.*

In the reduction and simplification of composed images, Meléndez went back to 17th century Italian and Dutch models of the school of Caravaggio, and shows influences from Velázquez, whom he undoubtedly observed with filial spirit. Thus the single source of light isolates and exalts every object with its own individual coloration, and scans the connection along the diagonal that meets the trihedral disposition of vases at the left. There is no lack of textural observation and sensitive taste for materials, especially in the meat of the salmon, the difference between the vessels, the translucent lemon peel. The immobile composition has authority and a silent density. It has been pondered and animated in terms of light and color and has a lasting, intense fascination. In pictures like this, Meléndez passed over the recent fashion for the Flemish taste or for Mario dei Fiori, as seen in such immediate precedents as the work of Juan de Arellano or Pérez, and returned to the models of Sanchez Cotan, Juan de Espinosa, Pedro de Camprobin and other artists of the first half of the 17th century.

LUIS EUGENIO MELÉNDEZ
Naples 1716; in Madrid from 1717; died in Madrid, 1780.
Still-life with Salmon and Lemon
Oil on canvas; 16 1/2″ × 28 3/4″. Signed on the edge of the table: *"L. Mz DºISº Pr Ano 1772."* Painted for Aranjuez, with a series of other canvases also in the Prado.

99

FRANCISCO DE GOYA Y LUCIENTES
Fuendetodos 1746; in Madrid 1763; in Italy
ca. 1770, Rome 1771; Madrid 1773; Painter
to the King 1786 and *Pintór de Camera* in

1789; in 1819 at *Quinta del Sordo;* exile in
Bordeaux from 1824; died in Bordeaux,
1828.

The Parasol
Oil on canvas; 3′5″ × 4′11 3/4″. Tapestry
cartoon for an over-door in the dining room
of El Pardo; executed on August 12, 1777.

FRANCISCO DE GOYA Y LUCIENTES. *The Parasol.*

By a wall, the elegant young Spanish girl sits in the sun, from which a *Maja* shades her with a green umbrella. With the tapestry cartoons of the same series, ordered from him by Charles III, this represents the first emergence of Goya's personality as a painter, reflecting in theme and background of woods and brush the French taste brought to Madrid by Houasse and even more the clear, fluent techniques of Giaquinto. It is a happy, sunny scene, with a gradation of colors which recalls the range of Tiepolo, especially in the abrupt dips in the blacks. In this and succeeding paintings, Goya's imagination is seen as luminously serene, in a climate without clouds or doubt, torment or pain; a manifestation of joy in life and a paean to its fullness and beauty.

FRANCISCO DE GOYA Y LUCIENTES. *Man Drinking.*

This is another scene of genre or Spanish manners, executed for the same series, and conceived and carried out by Goya in terms of contrasts between the various canvases. Compared to the preceding painting, this one has a more dramatic tone. Against a background sky that is equally clouded and vaporous stand the figures, at the edge of a wood traversed by rays of light that animate the colors. In theme there is recourse to Dutch genre scenes, but the technique is liquid, thin, pearly, with a fanciful and rich choice of colors that are concentrated in full sunlight, especially on the three figures of the *Majas* to the right.

FRANCISCO DE GOYA Y LUCIENTES
Man Drinking
Oil on canvas; 3'6" × 4'11 1/2".
Tapestry cartoon for an over-door in
the dining room of El Pardo;
executed on August 12, 1777.

FRANCISCO DE GOYA Y LUCIENTES
The Snowfall
Oil on canvas; 9'1/4" × 9'7 1/2". Cartoon
for a tapestry (which has been preserved),
painted for the El Pardo series at the end of
1786 or the beginning of 1787; sketch
(12 1/2" × 13") in the Silberman collection,
New York.

FRANCISCO DE GOYA Y LUCIENTES.   *The Snowfall.*
Some hunters and a dog followed by a mule loaded with a dead boar are
crossing a valley during a snowfall and a blizzard that is bending the bare
tree. Goya — with some suggestion of satisfied bravura — has played up
the general effect of the whites of the snow under the heavy grey sky, ma-
nipulating with careful calculation the thickening surfaces and the subtle
chromatic variations. The group, from the man in front with the gun to the
mule, has a forward movement that expands against the background with
its leveled surfaces. In the figures, especially the two to the left, the artist
works with extreme freedom of technique, fractioning the brushstrokes to
a degree of pointillism.

FRANCISCO DE GOYA Y LUCIENTES.   *The Flower Women.*
With the other canvases of the same series, this one represents a moment of
return, but with a more mature and personal command of pictorial language. The atmosphere is bright, the sun glorious, the countryside and the
hill already warm in the full springtime. The festive figures are caught ex-
changing flowers, while the countryman holds a baby rabbit in his hand.
The cycle to which this work belongs is developed predominantly in this
key of effusion and enjoyment of life. There are however episodes, such as
the *Injured Mason,* in a more severe and reflective tone, denser in composition, less relaxed in technique, with unexpected and impassioned passages.

FRANCISCO DE GOYA Y LUCIENTES
The Flower Women
Oil on canvas; 9'1 1/4" × 6'4". Painted after
June 29, 1786, for the "Dormitorio de los
Infantes Don Gabriel y Doña Maria Ana
Victoria" in the Escorial, where the tapestry
is preserved. A reduced version made by the
artist for Alameda de Osuna is today in the
Montellano collection, Madrid.

FRANCISCO DE GOYA Y LUCIENTES
Josefa Bayeu de Goya
Oil on canvas; 32″ × 22″. The identification
of the subject is traditional (she married
Goya in 1773, died in 1812). Acquired from
the Museo de la Trinidad in 1866.

FRANCISCO DE GOYAS Y LUCIENTES. *Josefa Bayeu de Goya.*
Composed according to a simple triangular distribution, the seated half-
length figure is mantled in tulle and has gold-embroidered sleeves. According to most critics the painting dates from 1798. It presents a moment of
sedate intimacy on the part of the artist, even if the forms do not lose their
pulsating animation. It is contained within a subtle range and technique,
concentrating on the meditative face and expression. The angular format is
traditional, but confers a tranquil, communicative quality on the figure. It
evidently was chosen so as to stay within a subdued, low-voiced key that
would not permit any distractions.

104

FRANCISCO DE GOYA Y LUCIENTES
San Isidro's Hermitage on His Feast Day
Oil on canvas; 16 1/2″ × 17 1/4″. Related,
like the *Meadow of San Isidro,* to a tapestry
cartoon on which Goya was working in May,
1788; paid for by the Duque de Osuna in
1799; Fernandez-Duran bequest (1930).

FRANCISCO DE GOYA Y LUCIENTES. *San Isidro's Hermitage on*
His Feast Day.

This sketch, like many others of the same period, continuing the first phase
of the artist's work, shows the growth of a more dramatic impetus, whose
stimulus is to be found as much in Magnasco as in Watteau. The layout
emphasizes his development; contrasts in size increase, points of view are
raised or lowered, light and shade are more clashing, the groups near and
distant are separated by spatial leaps. The technique is also more urgent
and fragmented, richer in clear-cut shadows; the brushwork is biting and
immediate, defining and accenting with a few essential touches, swift flicks
that break and agitate the silken ground of the colors.

FRANCISCO DE GOYA Y LUCIENTES. *The Nude Maja. pp. 106–107*
On a functional green ottoman, the *Maja,* disposed along a simple diagonal,
lies on silken cushions and finely worked sheets; her expression is more
naked than her beautiful body. It is one of the most disconcerting images in
all art, in which the exaltation of life in the feminine being is triumphant.
Goya completely identifies himself with this celebration of beauty, which is
not abstract nor an ideal canon, but an enthusiastic participation. The re-
splendent body lives in the embrace of the light, which seems to love her,
as in the ancient myth. The light is a mobile element in the room, and it
creates hollows of secret shadow and unexpected radiance; it dazzles and
skims, slips along the body and the textures of cloth, shines with palpita-

Pages 106–107:

FRANCISCO DE GOYA Y LUCIENTES
The Nude Maja
Oil on canvas; 3′2 1/4″ × 6′3″. Companion
piece to the following painting, and like it
painted during the years 1797–1798. In the
inventory of its owner, the royal favorite
Godoy, the two figures are called "Gypsies."
Formerly in the Academia de San Fernando;
in the Prado since 1901. Despite their strong
resemblances and the identical pose, perhaps
two different models were employed.